EARTH'S PRECIOUS

WATER

WATER CONSUMPTION AND SCARCITY

by John Perritano

Go to **www.openlightbox.com**, and enter this book's unique code.

ACCESS CODE

LBXX9426

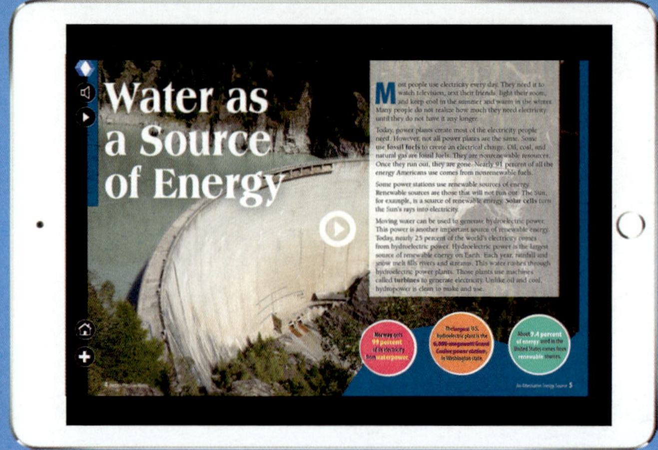

Lightbox is an all-inclusive digital solution for the teaching and learning of curriculum topics in an original, groundbreaking way. Lightbox is based on National Curriculum Standards.

STANDARD FEATURES OF LIGHTBOX

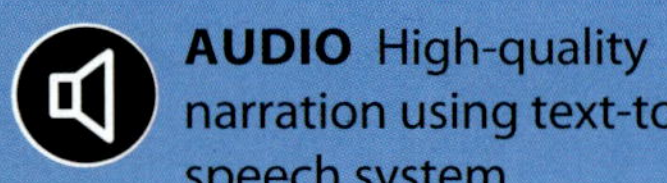
AUDIO High-quality narration using text-to-speech system

ACTIVITIES Printable PDFs that can be emailed and graded

SLIDESHOWS Pictorial overviews of key concepts

VIDEOS Embedded high-definition video clips

WEBLINKS Curated links to external, child-safe resources

TRANSPARENCIES Step-by-step layering of maps, diagrams, charts, and timelines

INTERACTIVE MAPS Interactive maps and aerial satellite imagery

QUIZZES Ten multiple choice questions that are automatically graded and emailed for teacher assessment

KEY WORDS Matching key concepts to their definitions

Contents

Usable Water

Water is the most important **natural resource** on the planet. Human life would not exist without water—specifically the fresh water that people drink. However, people take water for granted. They waste it and throw garbage into it. People also use too much water. As the world's population grows, there may one day come a time when there is not enough fresh water for humanity.

How can that be, if water is all around us? Water is plentiful. If scientists could build a drinking glass as large as the United States and fill it with every drop of water on the planet, the glass would be 90 miles (144.84 kilometers) tall. With all this water, it would seem like everyone should have enough to drink.

However, most of the world's water is salt water. While many fish and aquatic plants thrive in saltwater environments, humans cannot drink it or cook with it. They cannot water crops with salt water, as the plants would die. Only about 3 percent of all the water on Earth is suitable for drinking and growing crops. Of that, nearly 2 percent is locked away in polar ice or trapped in underground rock layers called aquifers.

Fresh water is becoming hard to find. As the world population climbs, water use is on the rise. In addition, climate change, including the gradual increase in Earth's surface temperature, impacts freshwater resources. Without changes in how people consume water, all the usable fresh water on the planet may one day disappear.

There is about **8.4 million** cubic miles (35 million cubic km) of usable fresh water on the planet.

The **7 billion** people who live on Earth can only use about **1 percent** of the world's water supply.

96.5 percent of Earth's water is found in the oceans.

Where is Water Scarce?

About 1.1 billion people do not have access to clean water. More than double that number cannot find clean water to drink for at least one month of each year. Clean water is vital for good health. Without it, people can get sick. Those that do not have access to clean water can be stricken with illnesses including **cholera** and **typhoid**.

Making sure people have enough clean water to drink is a priority for every nation. Yet, finding clean water is often hard, especially in poor countries in Africa, Asia, and South America. Why do some areas have more clean water than other areas? In some parts of the world, water is physically scarce. Desert locations or areas that receive little rain may have few usable water sources. That means the demand for water exceeds the land's ability to produce it. Climate change and human activities can also make water rare in these areas.

In other areas, people do not have enough clean water because of war, **economics**, or political conflicts. This is known as economic scarcity. Economic scarcity impacts about 1.6 billion people around the globe. Poor people living in slums pay 5 to 10 times more per unit of water than people living in wealthier neighborhoods.

About 70 percent of Haitians do not have access to clean water.

Water-borne illnesses cause more than half of the deaths in Haiti every year.

Most rural water sources in Haiti are contaminated. This is because there is no treatment system to cleanse water.

Haiti Water Crisis

When: Present | **Where:** Haiti

In Haiti, an island nation in the Caribbean, clean water is precious. Many people have to travel to garbage-filled rivers to get enough water for drinking and cooking. Still, groups are trying to help. They are repairing wells and providing thousands with clean water to drink. Schools and hospitals are slowly getting clean water. Communities across Haiti are trying to combat epidemics of cholera and typhoid by cleansing freshwater with chlorine to kill germs and bacteria.

DISCUSSION

What factors may explain why clean water is scarce in Haiti? Explain how these are similar to and different from the area where you live. Why is it similar or different?

Haiti is the poorest nation in the Western Hemisphere.

About 54 percent of Haiti's population lives on less than $1 a day.

Water scarcity became much worse in Haiti after a large earthquake in 2010.

California has more than 900 wastewater treatment plants and 100,000 miles (160,934 km) of sanitary sewers that manage about 4 billion gallons (15.1 billion liters) of wastewater generated each day.

Water Treatment

The United States is one of the safest places to drink a glass of water. Most U.S. cities and towns rely on public water systems. The treatment plant is at the heart of those systems. Typically, if drinking water is pumped from lakes, rivers, streams, or ponds it requires more treatment than water pumped from an underground aquifer. This is because surface water often contains more **contaminants** than an underground source.

Water treatment plants can use several methods to cleanse water. Generally speaking, the first step is to add chemicals to water. These chemicals have a positive electrical charge. Dirt and other dissolved particles have a negative charge. When the chemicals touch the contaminants, the particles stick together. This forms larger particles known as floc. Floc is heavier than water. It sinks to the bottom of the treatment tank. That means the water on top of the tank is clear. Workers take that water and pass it through a series of filters.

The filters remove dust, parasites, bacteria, and other chemicals. Once the water is filtered, workers add more chemicals, such as chlorine, to the water. Those chemicals kill any remaining germs and bacteria.

To remove lightweight contaminants from wastewater, water treatment plants sometimes use rotating filters that skim the tops of water tanks.

Another way to cleanse water is to recycle wastewater used for washing or cleaning. In 2022, San Diego will open a water treatment plant that recycles this water. Countries such as Singapore, Australia, and Namibia have been using recycled water for years. There are a number of ways to recycle water. In general, sewer water goes through the same cleansing process as drinking water. Once the solids have been removed, however, workers add bacteria to the wastewater. The bacteria eats any remaining solids. As that happens, a second round of sludge settles to the bottom of the treatment tank. Filters remove whatever contaminants remain in the water at the top of the tank. Once that is completed, a third round of chemical cleansing takes place.

San Diego's new recycled water plant is expected to produce **30 million gallons** (1.1 billion liters) of water a day.

The plant **will provide 33 percent** of San Diego's **water supply**.

San Diego **currently pumps 85 percent of its water** from the Colorado River and Northern California.

Industrial and Agricultural Uses of Water

One cow drinks about 24 gallons (91 L) of water on a hot day.

It takes three years' worth of drinking water to manufacture a T-shirt. That is roughly 713 gallons (2,700 L). Food also requires water. An apple takes about 50 gallons (190 L) of water a day to grow. Without water, farms could not grow crops or water livestock. People would not have apples to eat or milk to drink. Without water, factories and businesses could not produce many goods and services, such as T-shirts and jeans.

On the farm, water comes from a variety of sources. Farmers pump water from rivers, streams, and canals. They may collect it from ponds, reservoirs, and lakes. Some farmers use water from wells, and a few collect rain water. Watering crops is called irrigation. Nearly 40 percent of the world's food supply is produced by irrigation. Moreover, 70 percent of all freshwater is used to produce food. In the United States, farmers irrigate roughly 55 million acres (22 million hectares) of farmland.

AGRICULTURAL WATER USE AROUND THE WORLD

The chart below reflects the percentage of total water withdraw for agricultural uses for selected countries.

Country	Percentage
Mali	97.86
Sudan	94.78
India	90.41
Saudi Arabia	88
Mexico	76.69
China	64.61
Brazil	54.59
United States	40.22
Russia	19.94

Paper production facilities use about 2.6 gallons (10 L) of water to produce one sheet of letter size paper.

Farmers in the western part of the United States use more water than those elsewhere in the country. However, **droughts** have affected large areas of the east. In recent years, the eastern part of the United States has greatly expanded the number of irrigated acres. Growing corn takes the most water, about 25 percent of the total U.S. irrigated acreage.

Industry uses its fair share of freshwater, too. Factories, mills, and other businesses use water for fabrication and to cool equipment. Industry uses water to wash goods and to transport them. Some of the biggest users of water include the paper industry, the chemical industry, the oil refining industry, and companies that process metals.

Impact of Overconsumption

Many humans take water for granted. It is often wasted. People also foul it by dumping hazardous chemicals, raw sewage, and other **toxins** into the environment as they use water. Chemicals are among the largest sources of water pollution. Animal and human waste can foul water, too. Waste from humans, pets and livestock contain disease-carrying bacteria that can get into the water supply.

Another environmental impact is when factories and power plants dump hot wastewater into rivers, lakes, and streams. Warm water makes it difficult for fish and plants to breathe. Large amounts of hot water being dumped into natural areas can cause fish and other aquatic wildlife to suffocate.

In modern power plants, water is boiled at high temperatures to produce steam. To replace evaporated water, power plants use about 14,126 cubic feet (400 cubic meters) of water per day.

The lack of fresh water caused by human overconsumption is turning some areas in North America into deserts. Many parts of Canada, Mexico and the United States have become extremely **arid** over the past several years. Today, about 40 percent of North America's cropland and rangeland have turned to desert.

Additionally, half of the world's wetlands have disappeared since 1900. These marshes, ponds, and swamps are home to many animal and plant species. Wetlands also protect against storms and floods. Some wetlands act as huge water filters, cleaning and protecting freshwater supplies. Still, people are draining wetlands to build factories, farms, and homes. As a result, water levels drop, and plants and animals die.

Danger on Lake Baikal

Lake Baikal is the world's deepest freshwater lake. Located in eastern Siberia, in Russia, the lake is home to thousands of animal and plant species. However, human activities, including climate change, overconsumption, and overuse, are threatening the lake. Its waters are warming much faster than the global average. That has had a devastating impact on the lake's ecosystem. Other human activities have also impacted the lake's health.

Sewage

Each year, boats and barges dump tons of liquid sewage into the lake. Moreover, at least 145 tons (132 metric tons) of sewage are pumped into the water from a popular vacation resort.

Dams

Scientists fear that six planned hydroelectric dams in Mongolia will impact the lake even more, disrupting the waterway's fragile ecosystem.

Algae Blooms

The increase in pollution has created devastating algae blooms. The algae take in oxygen from the water that fish need to survive. In 2014, 1,650 tons (1,500 metric tons) of algae washed up on the lake's shore.

Sludge

A portion of the lake is still contaminated with sludge produced by a paper mill that closed in 2013.

The Water Crisis

In 2018, the residents of Cape Town, South Africa, found themselves in the middle of a water crisis. At that time, the city was in danger of running out of fresh water. Three years of drought, the overbuilding of homes and businesses, and an old water delivery system had drained the city. The only things residents could do was to conserve, or save, water and to hope for rain. At one point, the city limited each person to 13.2 gallons (50 L) of water a day. The government also threatened to shut the water off for homes and businesses. The city was able to push back "Day Zero," the day the city would run out of water, to 2019.

The Cape Town water crisis is an example of what can happen when people overuse and abuse freshwater resources. It is also an example of how much water people can save when they put their minds to it.

During the Cape Town water crisis, residents were forced to collect their drinking water from emergency water stations.

What happened in Cape Town is expected to happen in other areas, including California, Brazil, and Spain. The global water crisis was fueled by many things over many years. The largest factor was the increase in the world's population. Within the last half century, the number of humans who inhabit the planet has more than doubled to 7.6 billion.

As the population grew, homes needed to be built, farms had to grow more food, and factories and businesses had to make more products. This impacted the water supply and forced millions to live without access to clean water. The increase in population also meant an increase in pollution and wasted water. About 60 percent of water used in farming is wasted because of leaky irrigation systems and poor application methods. In addition, farmers are growing crops that use too much water for their area.

In California, almond trees consume more water than any other crop, using about 10 percent of the state's agricultural water supply.

Moreover, the growing population has contributed to climate change. As a result, droughts are longer and hotter. Floods, hurricanes, and other storms may be more devastating. As Earth continues to warm, glaciers and ice packs, which hold an amazing amount of freshwater, are melting into the oceans, destroying even more valuable resources.

Experts predicted that the water crisis in **Cape Town will cost 300,000 farmers** their jobs.

On "Day Zero" officials in Cape Town will open **200 water-collection points** around the city.

To save water, **Hotels in Cape Town** informed guests that they could **only take 90-second showers**.

Hydrologists

Hydrologists are scientists that study water. They look at how water moves, how much is available, and how clean it is. Hydrologists study the types of chemicals that contaminate water. They study how water moves across Earth's **crust**.

Some hydrologists work in offices. Others work outside. They use computers to look at data and to make predictions. Many times, a hydrologist will take water samples from rivers and ponds. They then analyze the water, collect data, and write reports.

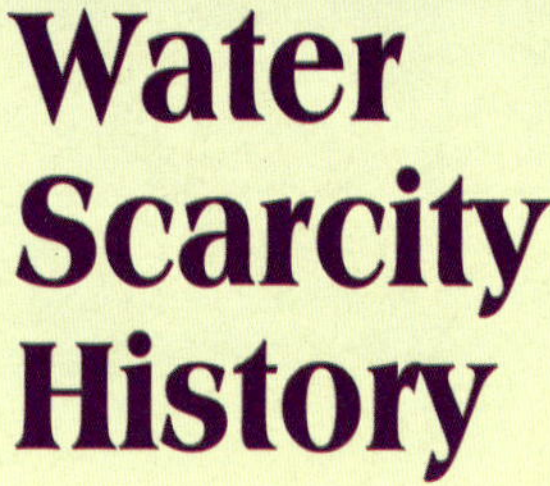

2011

The United Nations declared that a famine was underway in Somalia, a country in East Africa. The famine, UN officials said, was caused by one of the worst droughts in 60 years, coupled with political and religious unrest in the country.

1680

Pierre Perrault, a French scientist, investigates the origin of springs. He establishes the science of hydrology.

1993

The Hydrologic Research Center is founded in the United States. The organization performs and applies research relating to water use throughout the world.

Hydrologists look at how water influences the environment. They also try to understand how the environment impacts the quality and amount of water in an area. Some hydrologists study groundwater, while others study surface water. Hydrologists work closely with scientists who study the atmosphere and ecosystems.

Many hydrologists have master's degrees. Others have Ph.Ds. Most colleges and universities, however, do not offer specific hydrology degrees. Instead, colleges allow students to concentrate in hydrology while offering degrees in Earth science, engineering, and **geology**. Hydrologists need to be good in math, statistics, computers, and life science. They must also know the laws that impact the environment.

2015

A group of doctors urges the city of Flint, Michigan to stop using water from the Flint River. The doctors found high levels of lead, a toxic element, in the blood of children who drank water from the river.

2015

Governor Jerry Brown of California orders residents in the cities to reduce their use of water because of a years-long drought that has gripped the state.

2016

In May, Lake Mead, the largest human-made reservoir in the United States, reached its lowest point ever following years of drought in California and surrounding states. The water level fell to 1,074 feet (327 m).

Water Scarcity around the World

1 Lake Maracaibo, Venezuela

Lake Maracaibo is an ancient lake that is about 36 million years old. It is known for its beauty. Yet, it is also one of the most polluted lakes in the world. About 15,000 miles (24,000 km) of oil pipelines crisscross the lake. Many of those pipes leak, and oil has washed up on the lake's shore, harming fish and birds. Additionally, many companies dump waste into the waterways that run into the lake.

2 Buendia Dam, Spain

During the past 20 years, Spain has lost 20 percent of its freshwater. Experts say that number will rise to 25 percent by 2021. The country's farmers use 80 percent of Spain's freshwater resources to irrigate cropland. Water loss has also affected the country's electricity industry. The Buendia Dam, along with three others, has experienced lower water levels due to major droughts.

3 Nairobi, Kenya

In southern African countries, more than 319 million people do not have access to reliable drinking water. About 102 million people out of 159 million rely on surface water. Increasing populations also cause problems with water supplies. The water system in Nairobi, Kenya, was designed for about 500,000 people. Today, it provides water to a population of 4 million.

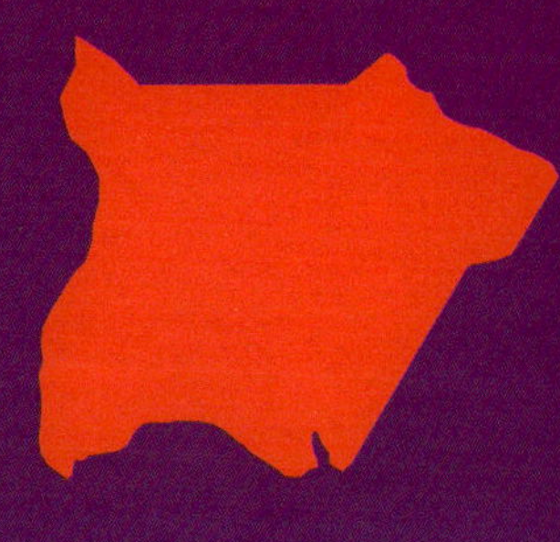

4 Lake Baikal, Russia

Russia is home to 25 percent of the world's freshwater supply, including Lake Baikal. However, about 75 percent of this water is polluted by industrial waste. In 2017, Russia's ministry of Natural Resources stated that 40 percent of Russians consumed water that is unhealthy to drink.

5 Bagalkot, India

More than 100 million people in India live in areas, such as the city of Bagalkot, where water quality is poor. These heavily-polluted cities produce 80 percent of the waste that pollutes the country's rivers. More than 600 million are at risk of having surface-water supply disrupted.

6 Ying River, China

The Ying River is one of the most polluted and dangerous waterways in the world. It has been polluted for more than a decade but children continue to play in the river, which often has pink foam on top. Today, this pollution has begun to pass into groundwater used by farmers for irrigation.

Water Consumption Issues

Water use is an important issue. Your town can have a problem with water and most people would not know. Research online or in the library how your community dealt with a water use problem. You can also talk to experts at a local museum, university, or local water department.

WHAT IS HAPPENING?

As you conduct your research, take notes on the specific problem. What were the specifics of the problem? What caused it? Who or what did it affect? Be as specific as you can.

WHAT WAS THE EFFECT?

Use newspaper articles and interviews to determine how the problem impacted people in the community. Were people without drinking water? Did water have to be transported in?

WHAT WAS THE OUTCOME?

Research the measures the community took to deal with the problem. Was the problem solved? Were any steps taken to make sure that it would not happen again? Are there any steps that could have been taken but were not? If so, why?

Measuring Water Use

Instructions

Step 1: Turn on the faucet just enough so it begins to drip. Place the bucket under the faucet and write down the time.

Step 2: Wait one hour. Using the measuring cup, record the amount of water that has dripped. Return the water to the bucket.

Step 3: After two hours, record the amount of water in the bucket again. Turn off the faucet and use the water to water a plant.

Step 4: Using the data for one and two hours, estimate how much water would leak from the faucet during a day and how much would be wasted during a week. What can this tell you about water conservation?

Faucet

Measuring cup

Bucket

Pen and paper

Quiz

Test your knowledge by answering these questions. All of the information can be found in the text you just read. The answers are provided below for easy reference.

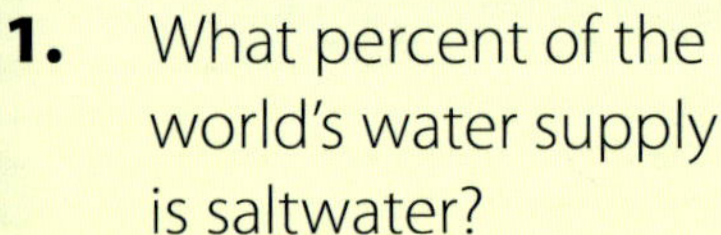

1. What percent of the world's water supply is saltwater?
2. What are aquifers?
3. What is the population of Earth?
4. What is water treatment?
5. What is floc?
6. What is the main water supply for the American Southwest?
7. How many acres of farmland in the United States are irrigated?
8. What percent of the world's available freshwater is used for agriculture?
9. Which South African city is running out of water?
10. What is a major cause of pollution on Lake Maracaibo?

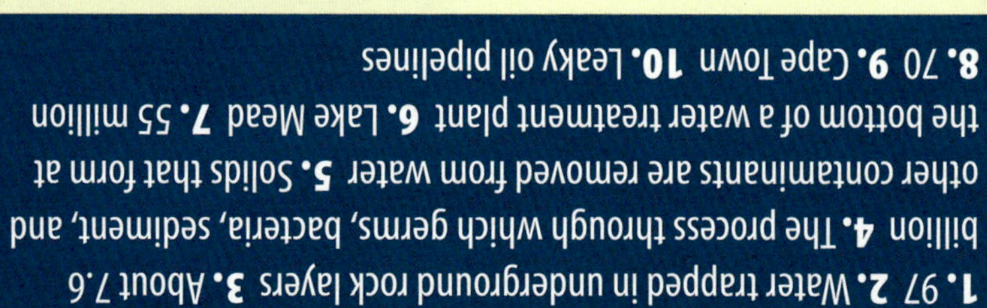

ANSWER KEY

1. 97 **2.** Water trapped in underground rock layers **3.** About 7.6 billion **4.** The process through which germs, bacteria, sediment, and other contaminants are removed from water **5.** Solids that form at the bottom of a water treatment plant **6.** Lake Mead **7.** 55 million **8.** 70 **9.** Cape Town **10.** Leaky oil pipelines

Key Words

arid: dry

cholera: infection of the small intestine caused by a waterborne bacterium

contaminants: substances that make something polluted

crust: the top most layer of Earth

droughts: prolonged periods of low precipitation that leads to shortages of water

economics: the system of how money is made and used in a particular country or region

geology: science that deals with Earth's physical structure, history, and the various processes that act on the planet

natural resource: a material or substance such as water, minerals, forests, oil, and coal that occur in nature and can be used for economic gain

toxins: poisonous substances

typhoid: an infectious bacterial fever that causes red spots on the chest and severe stomach pains

Index

LIGHTBOX

SUPPLEMENTARY RESOURCES

Click on the plus icon found in the bottom left corner of each spread to open additional teacher resources.

- Download and print the book's quizzes and activities
- Access curriculum correlations
- Explore additional web applications that enhance the Lightbox experience

LIGHTBOX DIGITAL TITLES
Packed full of integrated media

VIDEOS

INTERACTIVE MAPS

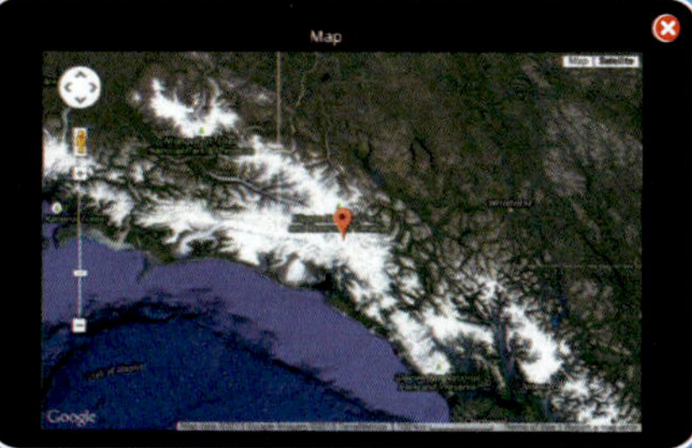

WEBLINKS

SLIDESHOWS

QUIZZES

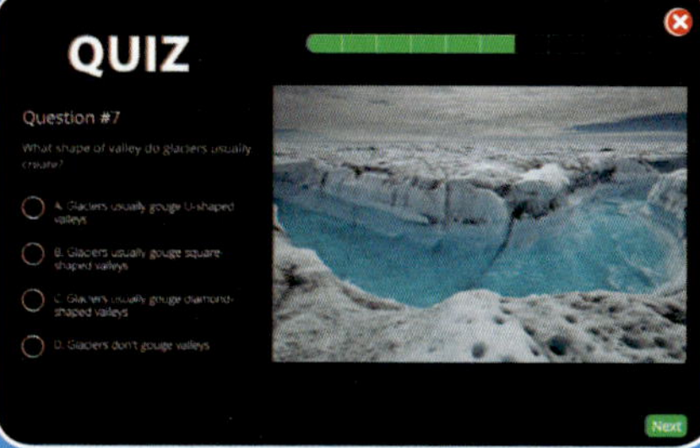

OPTIMIZED FOR
- ✓ TABLETS
- ✓ WHITEBOARDS
- ✓ COMPUTERS
- ✓ AND MUCH MORE!

Published by Smartbook Media Inc.
350 5th Avenue, 59th Floor
New York, NY 10118
Website: www.openlightbox.com

Library of Congress Control Number: 2018944577

ISBN 978-1-5105-3893-1 (hardcover)
ISBN 978-1-5105-3894-8 (multi-user eBook)

Printed in Brainerd, Minnesota, United States
1 2 3 4 5 6 7 8 9 0 22 21 20 19 18

072018
120517

Project Coordinator John Willis
Art Director Terry Paulhus

Photo Credits
Every reasonable effort has been made to trace ownership and to obtain permission to reprint copyright material. The publisher would be pleased to have any errors or omissions brought to its attention so that they may be corrected in subsequent printings. The publisher acknowledges Alamy, Getty Images, iStock, and Shutterstock as its primary image suppliers for this title.